Scientific Significance of Indian Festivals

By

Dr. Ravi Prakash Arya

AMAZON BOOKS, USA

In association with

INDIAN FOUNDATION FOR VEDIC SCIENCE
1051, Sector-1, Rohtak-124001, Haryana, India
Ph. Nos. + 91 9313033917; + 91 9650183260
Emails: vedicscience@rediffmail.com
vedicscience@hotmail.com
www.vediscience.net

First Edition

Kali era: 5019 (c. 2017)
Kalpa era: 1,97,29,49,119
Brahma era: 15,50,21,97,9,49,119

ISBN No. 81-87710-72-1

Table of Contents

1

Science of Śiva and Śivarātrī

Śiva has a great significance in *Paurāṇika* mythology and cultural tradition of Bharata. *Paurāṇika* mythology is nothing else but the figurative description of the cosmic/natural history. *Paurāṇika* symbolism provides us numerous clues to understanding the process of creation. If we call Vedas as depicting the science of creation, *Paurāṇas* may be called as depicting the history of creation. That is why it has been verily stated in the Vedic tradition - *ithāsa purāṇābhyām vedam samupabṛṅhayeta*. 'That is Veda can be further elaborated with the help of *Itihāsa* and *Purāṇa*.' Here *Itihāsa* or *Purāṇa* do not signify some political or social history of mankind, but the history of creation is signified by the terms *Itihāsa* and *Purāṇa*. That is why a lot of confusion has created. We are confusing the names of human history with the names of natural or cosmic history, there being the similarity of names between the two. So-called Paurāṇika mythical names do not represent the human beings, but cosmic beings. Here it may also be made clear that there is a difference between *Paurāṇika* mythology and the mythologies of the rest of the world. Vedic mythology is not the mythology in the real sense. Entire *Pauraṇika* mythology symbolises some scientific truth behind it, whereas the mythologies of the rest of the world either represent their distorted picture of *Purāṇika* mythology, being borrowed from Bharat by its migratory people to the place of their migration or the mere mythical speculations. Under the circumstances, when Vedas or Purāṇas talk about the Śiva or Viṣṇu, we generally take them to mean human beings or the characters of human history. However, the fact remains that they are names of some natural or cosmic phenomena. Śiva is often endowed with the attributive epithets like Candramauli or Śaśīśekhar (having a crescent moon over his forehead). We are also aware that the night of the fourteenth of the dark half of every lunar month is called Śivarātri (night of Śiva). Here Śiva represents Sun. This is why the phenomenon *rātri* or night is assigned to him as *Śivarātrī.* In the dawn of fourteenth of the dark half, we have the last visibility of the moon rising in the east, which is followed by the rising Sun. So the Sun of that morning rises with the crescent moon over his forehead. This spectacle can be observed only at the dawn following *Śivarātrī*, the appellation *Śivarātrī* for that night and appellation of *Candramauli* or *Śaśīśekhara* for the rising sun is the most appropriate.

Having understood the significance of *Śivarātri* of every lunar month, it becomes clear that *Mahāśivarātrī* must represent the longest *Śivarātrī* (night of the rising sun) of the year, which would naturally be closest to the winter solstice. As such *Mārgaśīrṣa Kṛṣṇa Caturdaśī*, i.e. the fourteenth of the dark half of *Mārgaśrṣa* will be called *Mahāśivarātrī.* But presently as inherited through tradition, this festival is celebrated on ***Phālguna Kṛṣṇa Caturdaśī* on 6th March**. This indicates that at the time of commencement of this festival called *Mahāśivarātrī,* winter solstice would have occurred close to the dark half of *Phālaguna* on 22 Feb. Today *Kṛṣṇa Caturdaśī* that falls close to winter solstice belongs to *Mārgaśīrṣ a* month and falls on **26 November**. This gives the precession of 4 **(Nov.) + 31 (Dec.) + 31 (Jan.) + 22 Feb = 88** days. One day's precession takes place in 72 days. So one can easily calculate that the present date of the festival of *Mahāśevarātrī* was fixed around 88 x 72= 6336 years before or 1233 years before *Kali* era or 1294768th year of *Tretā* or say that 4333 BC. So this is how the truth behind Candramauli Śiva and *Mahāśivarātrī* goes. Having understood the significance of the *Śivarātrī* of every lunar month, it becomes clear that *Mahāśivarātrī* must represent the longest *Śivarātrī* (night of rising sun) of the year, which would naturally be close to winter solstice.

2

Science of Śrāddha and Pitṛpakṣa

The *Śrāddha pakṣa* or *Pitṛpakṣa* is beginning from 15th Sept. or say with the beginning of dark half of Āśvina Month. The ending period of *Śrāddha pakṣa* or *Pitṛpakṣa* is known as *Pitara Visarjana*. This period is celebrated as the period for remembering and showing respect to the departed souls in Indian families. This period is also enumerated as inauspicious day. People keep away from purchasing new things and making other significant purchases. But nobody knows the science behind this phenomenon. We all are celebrating this period through ages, knowing not why. As it has already been observed by the author of present lines that almost each and every tradition in India has a sense and science behind it. Nothing became prevalent in this country of great sages and Vedas out of dogmas. In middle age, we forget the actual significance behind these rituals and started to celebrate them in a superstitious manner.

The tradition of *Śrāddha pakṣa* or *Pitṛpakṣa* also shows a great scientific awareness of Vedic people. The concept of *Śrāddha pakṣa* or *Pitṛpakṣa* is associated with the Vedic time reckoning system. As per astronomical time reckoning system of the Vedas, the time has been divided into several units ranging from smallest to the biggest one as per the various movements of satellites, planets, and stars. Among those time units are *Uttarāyaṇa*, *Dakṣiṇāyana* and *Devayāna* and *Pitṛyāna*. *Uttarāyaṇa* and *Dak-ṣiṇāyana* are quite famous. All of us know that *Uttarāyaṇa* is the inclination of Northern hemisphere of earth towards Sun, and *Dakṣiṇāyana* is the tendency of Southern hemisphere of earth towards the sun. In the beginning of the present *Kalpa* and even 2160 years ago, *Uttarāyaṇa* use to fall with *Makara Saṅkrānti* and *Dakṣiṇāyana* with *Karka Saṅkrānti.* Accordingly, present Calendar was updated by Aryabhaṭa 1637years ago. Since the time of Aryabhaṭa Indian Calendar makers are following his amended calendar, without giving due regard to the time of precession lapsed since his days. These days *Makara Saṅkrānti* is celebrated after the pattern of Aryabhaṭa's calendar on the first day of bright half of *Pauṣa māsa* (14th January). Whereas actual *Makara Saṅkrānti* starts on 21st Dec. 14th January falls in the middle of *Makara Saṅkrānti.* Similarly the actual Uttarāyaṇa today falls on 21st December. Thus the period of Uttarāyaṇa has also slid 1692 years back. In fact, the calendar of the universe requires updating every 72 years in the league with the precession of the equinox. So going by the precession, actual *Makara Saṅkrānti* takes place on 21st December and actual *Uttarāyaṇa* falls now on 21st December. Similarly, historical *Dakṣ iṇāyana* is not coinciding with *Karka Saṅkrānti.* Historical *Karka Saṅkrāti* falls during *Mithun Saṅkrānti* on 21st June. Astronomical *Dakṣiṇāyana* falls on 21st June which is the actual *Karka Saṅkrānti.*

The next important unit of time is *Devayāna* and *Pitṛyāna*. *Devayāna* and *Pitṛyāna* are less known and scarcely used time units. Though the Vedic scientists mentioned *Devayāna* and *Pitṛyāna* as two different paths. *Devayāna* path has a great importance, It has been said that: *Devayāno panthā vitatā mahāntaḥ*, i.e the path of *Devayāna* is more wide and open. In the Vedic tradition, *Devayāna* is identified with Sun's presence in the northern hemisphere and *Pitṛyāna* was identified with the sun's presence in the southern hemisphere of the earth. These days the sun remains present in the northern hemisphere of the earth for six months, i.e. from 21st of March till 22nd Sept. and in the southern hemisphere from 22nd Sept. to 21st March. So these days *Devayāna* period occurs from 21st March to 22nd Sept. and *Pitṛyāna* period from 22nd Sept. to 21st March.

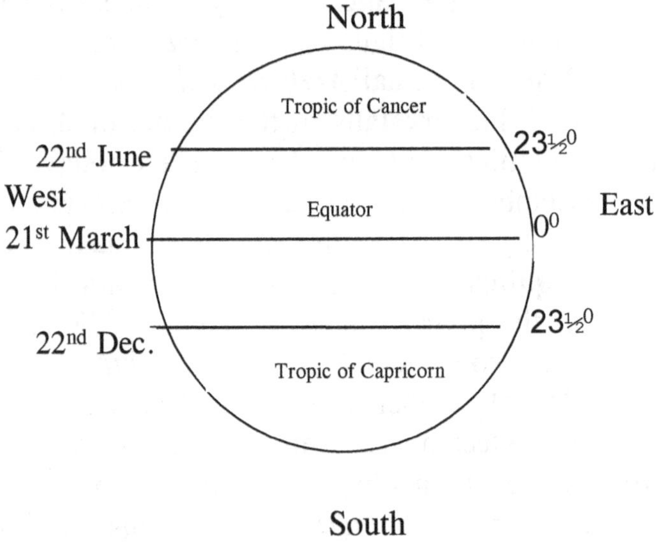

The tradition of celebrating *Śrāddha pakṣa* or *Pitṛpakṣa* was associated with this astronomical phenomenon. *Śrāddha pakṣa* or *Pitṛpakṣa* was celebrated as a mark of the end of the *Pitṛyāna* period. That is why this ceremony or ritual is known as *Pitara Visarjana*. Now the question is that why this period has been associated with the departed souls or the late ancestors of the families. This was the result of great scientific awareness in the Vedic period. In the Vedic period, the seers were well aware of the magnetism of the earth and the magnetism of animate beings, particularly human beings. The magnetic current of the earth flows from the North to South, thus *sumeru* acted as the North Pole of the earth's magnetism and *kumeru* acted as the south pole of earth's magnetism. Similarly, head of the human beings was discovered as the North Pole and legs as South pole. North pole of the Earth coincides with the Head as a North pole of a human beings and South pole of the Earth coincides with the legs as the south pole of the human beings. In other words, the alignment of the atoms is from North to South. It was also commonly known factor that the equal poles of a magnet repel each other and opposite poles attract each other. In fact, repelling of similar poles takes place because of collision of oppositely moving atoms. If the opposite poles put together, there will be no collision, since they keep running in the same direction. The distraction or collision is the sign of destruction or death and attraction or alignment is the sign of life. If there is an alignment of forces, there is a life. If the alignment is disturbed and collision takes place, the destruction or death bell is alarmed. Owing to the above fact, Head (North pole) of human beings cannot go with the North Pole of the earth, since the magnetic alignment of the human body and earth is disturbed which leads to several biological and psychological disturbances in human beings leading to their early end. Legs (South pole) of human beings can go with the North pole of the earth. As such there was a rule in the Vedic tradition (which is still followed in Indian tradition) that a person should sleep with his head either pointing to South or West (i.e. facing either to North or East) thus allowing the North pole of the human-beings going with the south pole of the earth and south pole of human beings going to the North Pole of the earth. In North Indian tradition (which is still practised), when a person dies he is placed with his head facing Northward, thus placing the similar pole together as a symbol of death. When a person is alive, his legs go Northward and when he dies his legs go to Southward. Keeping in view of this phenomenon, South direction and southern hemisphere was declared as the direction of *pitaras* (deads) and *Pitara loka.* Similarly, North direction and Northern hemisphere of the Earth was declared as the direction of *Devas* and *Deva loka.* That is why Sun's presence in the northern hemisphere was called as *Devayāna* and in the southern hemisphere of the earth as *Pitṛyāna.* In the same chain, *Pitṛpakṣa* was celebrated to mark the end of the *Pitṛyāna* period as well as a symbol of the dead persons in the families. That is why, *Pitṛpakṣa* was also called *Śrāddha pakṣa* (fortnight to mark the respect for dead). It was all symbolic and nothing to do with any kind of rituals or auspiciousness and inauspiciousness. The concept of taking *Devayāna* as an auspicious period and *Pitṛyāna* as inauspicious was solely based upon the greater period of light and greater period of darkness. The period of light was associated with life and darkness with death. Vedic culture is the culture of light, enlightenment. Light also symbolises knowledge, whereas darkness symbolises ignorance. Vedic seers were the worshipers of knowledge and not of the darkness or material things. So *Devayāna* period was given preference over the period of *Pitṛyāna.* In view of the same a person surcharged with knowledge was considered as *Deva* (literally meaning 'illuminating'), or *Sura* (enlightened) and a person having no knowledge was called as *dānava* or *asura* (darkened with ignorance). Spiritually, an enlightened person was considered as living and ignorant as dead. A person who never tried to gain knowledge was considered as committing suicide, as the life force of soul is not physical food, but the knowledge. The *Īśa Upaniṣad* (Yajurveda, 40.3) says it in clear-cut terms:

asuryā nāma te lokā

andhena tamasāvṛtā

tans te pretya abhi-gacchanti

ye ke ca ātmahano janāḥ

'That is the species (of animals and birds), called as *asura lokas*, are achieved by those who kill their spirit by acquiring no knowledge'.

Thus the physically alive persons were also associated with the day or the sun and dead persons were associated with darkness or night. Since night is dominated by Moon, so the Moon was declared as the abode of deads. The physically deads are considered as living upon the surface of the moon in Indian folk tradition.

Here one more important fact to note is that these days sun remains present in the northern hemisphere of earth from 21st of March till 22nd Sept. and in the southern hemisphere from 22nd Sept. to 21st March. Accordingly, these days the actual end of *Pitṛyāna* takes place on 21st March, and so actual *śrāddha pakṣa* starts from the first day of dark half of month close to 21st March to the last day of the dark half or *Amāvaśyā* of that very month. On the other hand, according to the conventional view, *Pitṛyāna* period starts on **15th September with the first day of dark half of Āśvina** and ends on *Āśvina Amāvaśyā.* Thus according to these two different systems, we have two different *Navarātras* one falling close to March 21, i.e. first day of bright half of *Chaitra* and another falling close to 23rd September, i.e. first day of bright half of Āśvina. The former *Navarātra* goes by the actual updated system and the latter by the conventional (historical) one. One may raise a question here as to why there is the difference between the actual *Pitṛyāna* period and conventional one. The answer of this fact takes us back to the pretty remote history of Vedas and Vedic culture in India. Vedic history starts in India crores of years back even prior to the end of *Cākṣusa Manvantara* or the beginning of *Vaivasvata Manvantara* (around 12-13 crore years ago) when the Indian part of the globe was the part of the southern hemisphere and the north polarity was also in the south. Prior to the end of *Cākṣusa Manvantara* or the beginning of *Vaivasvata Manvantara* India was the part of the southern hemisphere and the north polarity was also in the south, the concept of *Devayāna* and *Pitṛyāna* was also based upon the sun's presence in the southern and northern hemispheres respectively. That is why Indian tradition is using both the measurements, a historical one and the current one. To preserve the crores of years old history of Vedic tradition, the conventional way of celebrating the *Pitṛyāna* period is still going on. Thus we must understand the significance of both the *Navarātras* cited in the *Pañcāṅgas.* Actual *Navarātras* fall close to **21st of March, the first day of bright half of *Caitra* and historical *Navarātras* falls close to 22nd Sept.**, i.e. first day of bright half of *Āśvina.* The word *nava* in *Navarātras* is indicative of 'new' and 'nine'both. That is why *Navarātra* period is celebrated for nine days. Thus one can understand that *Śrāddha* or *Pitṛpakṣa* celebrated these days is wrong and has no significance. Their actual period is the dark half of *Caitra* close to 21st March. The way, they are celebrated is also wrong. This method also kills the actual meaning of the *Śrāddhas.*

***Pitṛpakṣa* and *Kanāgata*:** The period of *Pitṛpakṣ a* is also known as *kanāgata* in some parts of India. Actually, the beginning of historical *Pitṛpakṣa* generally takes place during sun's entry into *Kanyā* (Virgo) sign. Since the sun is *Kanyāgata* (entered into Virgo sign) in this period, this period is also known as *Kanāgata.*

The feasting of *Kanyās* (Virgins): Here it may also be noticed that the *Navarātra* celebrations end with the feast given to the *kanyās* (virgins). This tradition of feasting *kanyās* or virgins is also based upon the wrong notion of relating the term kanyā with virgins rather than the actual Virgo sign. The feasting of *kanyās* is variously pronounced as *kañjakas* etc. which is the degenerated form of *Kanyā* itself.

Thus it is clear from the foregoing, that *Pitṛpakṣa* or *Śrāddha* shows the Indian scientific tradition of time calculation system and have no religious or ethical colouring behind it as is considered the present day.

3

Astronomical Base of Vaishakhi/Bihu/Vishu/Naba Varsha/Bohaag/Varsha Pirappu

13th April is celebrated as *Vaishakhi* in Panjab. The same day is observed as 'Varush Pirappu' in Tamil Nadu, 'Rangoli Bihu' or 'Bohaag' in Assam. Similarly, April 14th is observed as 'Vishu' in Kerala and 'Poyala Baishakh' or 'Naba Varsh' in Bengal. 'Baishakh' month is taken as new agricultural year all over India. That is why this is called as a harvest festival. Since Bharat was an agricultural country, these festivals are closely related with Indian social life. Later these festivals assumed religious importance also. But still, their social relevance is much more than their religious importance except 'Baishakhi' for Sikhs in Panjab where 'Baishakhi' also marks the birth of Khalsa. Whatsoever be the social relevance or religious significance of these festivals, the great thing about them is that they all have a scientific astronomical base behind them. These festivals not only mark the agriculture new year but also relate the centuries-old history of their origin as an astronomical new year on a scientific footing. The various names given to 'Baishakhi' festival in various parts of India as indicated above point out but one fact and that centuries ago this period was actually the new year day. The new year day in India astronomically is observed during '*Vasant sampāt*' (vernal equinox) when Sun is overhead the equator forming an angle of 90^0. These days this happens on 21st March. Here it may also be pointed out that the equator is called as '*Viṣuva vṛtta*' or '*Viṣuva*' in Vedic language. Thus 'Baishakhi' celebrations all over India in different names indicate the years old history of origin of these festivals of India when astronomical New year day of India based upon Vernal equinox use to fall on *Vaiśākha Śukla Pratipadā* instead of *Caitra Śukla Pratipadā* which is still being celebrated as New year owing to the historical significance of the origin of first New year on this earth on the day of *Caitra Śukla Pratipadā*. Actually some 864 years ago Vernal equinox use to take place on *Caitra Śukla pratipadā* **(6.4.2008)**. Now - a - days it has slid **16 days back on 21.3.2006**. Taking the precession of 1^0 into 72 years into account, one can easily calculate this period to be 16 x 72=1152 years ago. But the above festivals based upon the astronomical phenomenon of Vernal equinox taking place on *Vaiśākha Śukla Pratipadā* (i.e. 13 Aprill) tells an old history of their origin as a New astronomical year based upon Vernal Equinox. The time between 6th **April and 6th May comes to be about 30 days** which shows precession of **30** days. Thus the **2160 years ago** Vernal equinox use to fall on *Vaiśākha Śukla Pratipadā* and the same was celebrated as New year day. The above-cited festivals have 3000 years old memory. In fact, Baishakhi, the festival of Panjab is nothing else but the memory of 3000 years old New Indian year. Similarly 'Varush Pairuppu' of Tamil Nadu originated from the term Varsh Pratipada and points out the memory of 2000 years old astronomical phenomenon and New year thereof. Poyala Baishakh 'first Vaiśākha' or Nab Varsha '*Nava Varṣa*' of Bengal also point to 2000 years old Pratipada of Baishakh and New year day. 'Vishu' of Kerala originated from the Vedic term Vishuva meaning 'equator'. Since Indian new year starts with Sun overhead the Vishuva or equator. So Keralite 'Vishu' points to the Vishuva based 2000 old new year of *Vaiśākha Pratipadā.* The word 'Bihu' in 'Rangoli Bihu' or Bohaag of Assam are also the forms of 'Vishu'. 'Vishu' became 'Bishu' and 'Bishu' converted into 'Bihu' linguistically. Thus all these differently named festivals of different parts of India point out one and the same origin. This similarity is also the pointer to the integrated India 2000 years back. There was oneness and cultural and social similarity throughout India even in the days of yore. This fact also points out that Indian traditions and festivals have an astronomical and scientific base behind their development.

4

Diwali: The Festival of Lights

Diwali or Deepavali festival (literally meaning a row of lights/lamps) needs no introduction. It is known the world over as the festival of lights. In India, it is by far the most well known, popular and widely celebrated festivals. Because of the overwhelming diversity in terms of cultures, languages and traditions in India, every region has its own unique and distinct style of festivals.

Diwali or Deepavali is one festival which is celebrated all over India with equal gusto. The difference or disparity lies in the significance that is attached to this Indian festival in various parts of the country. For instance in North India, Diwali is essentially celebrated to mark the return of Lord Rama from his fourteen-year-long exile back to his kingdom of Avadh (Ayodhya).

In other parts of North India, especially in Bengal, Diwali assumes a strong element of Durga or Kali worship after Sita, wife of Rama. Despite the pan-Indianness of the festival, the fact remains that it is an occasion where people from different regions celebrate it to reveare some astronomical or historical phenomenon of Bharat.

Origins of Diwali

There are various accounts of the origins of the

Diwali-the festival of lights. In North India, the dominant belief about its origins connects it to the return of Lord Rama from his 14-year long exile. It is said that the practice started in the kingdom of Avadh, the seat of King Dashrath, father of Lord Rama.

The first day of Diwali commemorates the last day of Lord Rama's exile. By a royal decree, the kingdom of Avadh and all nearby provinces were illuminated by countless diyas to celebrate Rama's arrival on flying Vimana back. In other parts of northern India, for instance, in the Bengali-speaking areas, Diwali is celebrated to revere Sita in the name of Durga or Kali. Sita is remembered as the goddess of power who was responsible for the killing of the evil forces. In Bengal, this day is also known as the *Kāla Chaturdasi* or *Kāli Chaudas.* In South India, Diwali has a different significance. It marks the celebration of another historical victory-namely that of Lord Krishna over Asura Naraka, a western king who had held sixteen thousand daughters of various sages and Northern people in captivity. Later it was also associated with festivals associated with harvest.

Over the years, Diwali marked the beginning of financial year. And again, perhaps, for this reason, goddess Laxmi, who is the Goddess of wealth and prosperity, has come to be the presiding deity of Diwali.

Legends and myths attributed to genesis of Diwali

Etymologically the word Diwali has Sanskrit roots. In Sanskrit, it was originally Deepavali. Deepa means light and Avali means an array or a row, so quite literally Diwali means "a row of lights". In the Vedic calendar, which is Lunisolar one, it falls on *Amāvasyā*, or the new moon, about twenty days after the festival of Dussehra, in the month of Kārtika. Diwali has become a five-day Indian festival (*parva-utsava*), each day being dedicated to the celebration of some or other historical phenomenon. *Dhanwantari Triyodaśī*, also known as *Dhan teras* is the first day of Diwali. On this day, Lord Dhanwantari, physician par excellence, was born who propagated Ayurveda. Later mistakenly this day of *Dhana teras* was associated with money (Dhana meaning wealth). To support this wrong view some legends were also fabricated and since then people buy some new utensil to celebrate *Dhana teras.* This day should be celebrated as the birthday of Dhanawantari.

Narak Chaturdasi is the second day of Diwali festivities. It is also called *Choti Diwali* (Small Diwali). The significance of this particular day can be traced to the triumph of Lord Krishna over the western king Naraka - who had overwhelmed Indra in a battle. Lord Krishna battled Narakasura, defeated him, and set the captive women free. Diwali commemorates Lord Krishna's victory over Narakāsura.

Laxmi pujā: The third day is more popularly known as Lakshmi Puja. The concept of Lakshmi Puja is associated with the homecoming of Sita. In later days Lakshmi considered as the Goddess of wealth, so the people started worshipping wealth this day. So this day is mistakenly dedicated to goddess Laxmi who is considered as the goddess of Wealth.

This day is also celebrated in the form of another puja called the *Govardhan Puja.* It is in commemoration of Lord Krishna's rescue of the people of Gokul /Braja from the terrible wrath of Indra (flood). Lord Krishna lead the people of Braja to the mountain Govardhan to save them from the furry of the flood. This act of his earned him the sobriquet of Goverdhandhari, and also established his superiority. Goverdhan puja is offered as a tribute to Krishna's heroic feat. In parts of north India, people make cow dung replicas of the fabled mound, decorate it with flower petals and offer prayers. Another ritual also connected with this is the preparation of Anna koot or 'the mountain of food', a culinary potpourri prepared with more than hundred types of ingredients.

Bhai Duja: The fifth day of Diwali celebrations is devoted to the Brothers. According to history, on this day lord Yama, visited his sister Yamuna/ Yami and exchanged blessings with her as a gesture of brother to the sister. the practice continues today also. Brothers visit their sisters to exchange blessings from them.

5

Daśaharā (Dussehra)

Daśaharā is celebrated to commemorate the victory of Śri Rama over the Southern Chief Ravana. Ravana was killed on the 10th day of bright half of Iṣa (Āśvina) Month. The word *Daśaharā* is composed of two words *Daśa+ Harā.* Daśa means 'ten' and Harā means 'killed'. Thus the word Daśaharā means 'killed on 10th. It took ten days for Rama to kill Ravana. That is why Ravana was called as Daśānana or Daśagriva and the festival was called as Daśaharā. Later on, people mistakenly started translating the proper name of Daśānana or Daśagriva as 'Ten headed' and Daśaharā as a festival to commemorate the killing of 'Ten Headed'. It is all wrong and stupid notions. It may be known that a proper name can never be translated. The Proper name is a proper name, it cannot be explained by translation.

6

Basant Pañcamī

Basant pañcamī is celebrated to commemorate the *Basant* season. It is celebrated on the fifth day of the bright half of the month of the commencement of *Basant* season. Now *Basant* season falls in *Phālaguna*, so *Basant Pañcamī* should be celebrated on the fifth of the bright half of *Phālaguna* month. But we are still celebrating the historical *Basant Pañcamī* on the fifth of *Māgha Śukla.* If the time of precession is calculated from Phālaguna to Māgha (the backward calculation is done to find out the period of precession), there comes the precession of 330^0. I^0 precession takes place in 72 years. So 330-degree precession needs the period of 330x 72 = 23760 years. We can say that the festival of *Basant Pañcamī* was first introduced in India Some 23760 years ago. Still, we are celebrating the historical *Basant Pañcamī* on the fifth of *Māgha Śukla.* Actual astronomical *Basant Pañcamī* falls on the fifth of the bright half of *Phālaguna* month.

7

Makara Saṅkranti

Sun's transition from one Zodiac sign to another Zodiac sign is called *Saṅkranti.* For example, Sun's entry into *Makara* sign is known as *Makara Saṅkranti* which marks the commencement of Uttarāuaṇ. These days the sun enters in Makara sign on 22nd December, as such, astronomically *Makara Saṅkrānti* should be celebrated on 22nd December. But we celebrate it on 14th January. The reason behind it is that the present Indian calendar was lastly updated some 1700 years ago during the Siddhāntic period by Āryabhaṭṭa taking precession of earth into account. Here it may be pointed out that Earth's equinox precedes one degree every 72 years and so the calendar needs to be updated every 72 years. Since the time of Āryabhaṭṭa the calendar has receded 23.5^0 behind requiring an urgent update in league with the precession of the equinox. So going by the precession, actual *Makara Saṅkrānti* takes place on 22nd December and if we go by the un-updated calculations, then *Makara Saṅkrānti* will take place on 14th January. The updated calculations in the calendar are known as *Cala Gaṇanā* and static or un-updated calculations are known as *sthira* gaṇanā.

8

Viśvakarmā Day

Viśvakarmā day is celebrated on the first day of *Kārtika* Bright half to commemorate the birth of Viśvakarmā, the first Architect of the world.

9

Festival of Holi

(Vāsantī Navasasyeṣṭī)

Holi is celebrated in different corners of India with pomp and gaiety on full moon day in the month of Phālguna which is the month of March as per the Gregorian calendar. Thus Holi is celebrated in the Spring Season which is a period between the end of winter and advent of summer. We normally go through the transition phase of winter and summer. The period induces the growth of bacteria in the atmosphere as well as in the body. According to the Vedic seers during seasonal junctions we experience a change in our metabolism owing to the change in seasons. The equilibrium of *Vāta*, *Pitta*, *Kapha* is disturbed and we become vulnerable to diseases. *Kauṣitaki Brāhamaṇa* (5.1) points out this fact as : *bhaiṣajya-yajñā vā ete yaccāturmāsyāni. tasmād ṛtusandhiṣu prayujyante. ṛtusandhiṣu hi vyādhirjāyate.* 'That is these *Cāturmasya yajñas* are known as medicational *yajñas*. That is why they are performed during the seasonal junctions since the diseases are caused due to the change in seasons. So the knowledge of Seasonal junctions are very important to save us from the attack of viruses and thereby viral diseases by following a particular type of food regimen, cleansing, nourishing and securing body as well as performing *Cāturmāsya Yajñas.*

India is also the agricultural country. So her festivals are linked to the various harvesting seasons. The festival of Holi is linked to summer harvesting season. At the time of new harvesting time, people are very happy and make merry. According to Indian culture, when the season's first crop is harvested, the first fresh grain is offered to the deities. Agni or fire is said to be the mouth of the deities. So oblation of first harvested grain is given to the Navasasyeṣṭi yajña. The fresh grain is roasted and distributed among friends. This is also a symbol of community meals. These half roasted grains are known as 'Holaka' and so this festival is known as the festival of Holi or Holaka. This festival is also mistakenly associated with the Paurāṇika story of Prahllāda and Holikā.

According to the Vedic culture *kevalāgho bhavati kevalādi,* the one who eats alone is the sinner. So, Vedic culture advocates that feed other before to feed you. That is why in India, there is a tradition to organise the community meals and yajñas at the time of harvesting seasons. Indian culture is the culture of togetherness. The Vedas says *saha nāvavatu* (protect each other together), *saha nau bhunaktu* (eat together). This festival emphasises to be away from sinful acts and to live together.

10

Basoda

Basoda is celebrated as a main festival in many parts of North India such as Gujarat, Uttar Pradesh, Haryana and Rajasthan. This festival comes after Holi, it is usually marked on the 8th day after Holi and some communities celebrate this festival on the following Monday or Thursday after Holi. Basoda in Hindi is referred to 'Basi', which means stale, this festival is also known as Sheetla Ashtami.

A unique tradition is followed on the day of Basoda, people prefer to eat the food cooked on the previous day during this festival as they won't lit fire in their kitchens during this festival. Hence the families enjoy cold lunch as well as dinner. People worship Mata Sheetla on this festival and pray for the well-being of their family and to save their family from the upcoming harmful diseases in the following season. On this day, the food prepared one day before the festival is distributed as prasad (holy gift) in the temples. Thus Basoda is a unique festival celebrated by the North Indians. This festival is celebrated to signify the change in weather that is starting of the summer season. Basoda is celebrated by taking and distributing stale meals, not because of some dogma of superstition, but as a warning to the people that they may eat stale or Basi meals during the winter season, but the same is not advisable during the summer season, during summer season, stale meals become infected and adversely affect the health of body. So, Basoda is celebrated as a reminder to the common man in a society that use of stale meals is not advisable after a certain period of time keeping in view of the onset of the summer season.

11

Guru Pūrṇimā

Guru Pūrnima is observed on the full moon day of Āṣāḍha. This period falls after the commencement of Dakṣiṇāyana or winter solstice. This Parva is celebrated to commemorate the long intellectual tradition of Bharat started by Svayaṁbhū Brahmā in the beginning of the creation and resurrected and preserved by the Veda Vyāsa chair from time to time. So Āṣāḍha Pūrṇimā is known as Vyāsa Pūrnima. Since Guru as the main representative and custodian of this intellectual tradition used to impart Vedic knowledge to his disciples, Āṣāḍha Pūrṇimā was known as Guru Pūrnima. Veda Vyāsa Chair was also funded in ancient India to honour the Guru to preserve the knowledge of creation. We find the origin of the Chair from the very beginning of the present Vaivasvata Manvantara. As per ancient Indian tradition entire knowledge of the Vedas and other Śāstras vanishes with the passage of time by the conclusion of every Mahāyga (a period of 4,300,000 years). As such the lost knowledge is resurrected by high profile Ṛṣis who are destined to be born with the onset of the new Mahāyuga after a lapse of 4,300,000 years. This knowledge was taught by some particular Ṛṣis in the beginning of Mahāyuga, but after their death, the knowledge starts vanishing and with the onset of new Mahāyuga, those high profile Ṛṣis being reborn and the same lost knowledge is resurrected by them. This fact has been beautifully picturised by the tradition of Brahmāṇḍa Purāṇa (1.2.34.113) as under:

ये श्रुयन्ते दिवं प्राप्ताः ऋषयो ह्यूर्ध्वरेतसः।
मंत्र–ब्राह्मण–कर्त्तारः जायन्ते च युगक्षयात्।।

During the current Vaivasvata Manvantara, Veda Vyāsas are born every Dvāpara Yuga of a Mahāyuga. As such, till now 28 Mahāyugas of Vaivasvata Manvantara have elapsed, and so are 28 Dvāpara Yugas, as now we have 28th Kaliyuga going. So in the present Vaivasvata Manvantara, we have 28 Veda Vyāsas in tradition who resurrected this Vedic knowledge 28 times. *Brahmāṇḍa Purāṇa* (1.2.34.114-115) sheds ample good light on this fact as under:

एवमावर्तमानस्ते द्वापरेषु पुनः पुनः।
कल्पानामार्षविद्यानां नाना शास्त्रकृतश्च ये।।

वैवस्वतेऽन्तरे तस्मिन् द्वापरेषु पुनः पुनः।
अष्टाविंशतिकृत्वा वै वेदा व्यस्ता महर्षिभिः।।

Śaṅkarāchārya (in his commentary on Vedānta Darśana (1.3.30) support of the above-cited view of the Purāṇas and explains the same fact as:

युगान्तेऽन्तर्हितान् वेदान् सेतिहासान् महर्षयः।
लेभिरे तपसा पूर्वमनुज्ञाता स्वयंभुवा।।

The Vedic knowledge that vanishes after a period of a Mahāyuga is received by Maharishis along with its history through Samādhi. This knowledge was revealed to Svayambhū Brahmā in the beginning of creation.

Not only this, *Brahmāṇḍa Purāṇa* (1.2.34.114-115) has an exact record of 28 Veda Vyāsas who adorned the chair in various 28 Dvāpara Yugas of the present Manvantara.

1. The first Veda Vyāsa was named Svayaṁbhuva Veda Vyāsa. He was born in the first Dvāpara Yuga, i.e.

116,645,119 years ago.

2. The second was named Prajāpati, he was born in second Dvāpara yuga, i.e. 112,325,199 years ago.
3. The third Veda Vyāsa was named Uśanā Veda Vyāsa. He was born in the third Dvāpara Yuga, i.e. 108,005,119 years ago.
4. The fourth Veda Vyāsa was named Bṛhaspati Veda Vyāsa. He was born in the fourth Dvāpara Yuga, i.e. 103,685,119 years ago.
5. The fifth Veda Vyāsa was named Savitā Veda Vyāsa. He was born in the fifth Dvāpara Yuga, i.e. 96,365,119 years ago.
6. The sixth Veda Vyāsa was named Mṛtyu Veda Vyāsa. He was born in the sixth Dvāpara Yuga, i.e. 95,045,119 years ago.
7. The seventh Veda Vyāsa was named Indra Veda Vyāsa. He was born in the seventh Dvāpara Yuga, i.e. 90,735,119 years ago.
8. The eighth Veda Vyāsa was named Vasiṣṭha Veda Vyāsa. He was born in the eighth Dvāpara Yuga, i.e. 86,405,119 years ago.
9. Ninth Veda Vyāsa was Sārasvata, son of Saraswati. He was born in ninth Dvāpara Yuga, i.e. 82,085,119 years ago.
10. Tenth Veda Vyāsa was Tridhāmā. He was born in tenth Dvāpara Yuga, i.e. 77,765,119 years ago.
11. Eleventh Veda Vyāsa was Sārasvata, son of Saraswati. He was born in eleventh Dvāpara Yuga, i.e. 73,445,119 years ago.
12. In 12th Dvāpara Yuga, i.e. 69,125,119 years ago, Trivṛṣā became famous as 12th Veda Vyāsa.

13. In 13th Dvāpara Yuga, i.e. 64,805,119 years ago, Sanadvāja became famous as 12th Veda Vyāsa.

14. In 14th Dvāpara Yuga, i.e. 60,585,119 years ago, Antarikṣa held the famous Chair of 14th Veda Vyāsa.

15. In 15th Dvāpara Yuga, i.e. 56,165,119 years ago, Trayyāruṇi held the famous Chair of 15th Veda Vyāsa.

16. In 16th Dvāpara Yuga, i.e. 51,855,119 years ago, Dhananjaya held the famous Chair of 15th Veda Vyāsa.

17. In 17th Dvāpara Yuga, i.e. 47,525,119 years ago, Kṛtañjaya adorned the famous Chair of 17th Veda Vyāsa.

18. In 18th Dvāpara Yuga, i.e. 43,205,119 years ago, Ṛṣīja was crowned as 18th Veda Vyāsa.

19. In 19th Dvāpara Yuga, i.e. 38,845,119 years ago, Bharadvāja was crowned as 19th Veda Vyāsa.

20. In 20th Dvāpara Yuga, i.e. 34,565,119 years ago, Gautama, the son of Gotama was crowned as 20th Veda Vyāsa.

21. In 21st Dvāpara Yuga, i.e. 30,255,119 years ago, Uttama was crowned as 21st Veda Vyāsa.

22. In 22nd Dvāpara Yuga, i.e. 25,925,119 years ago, Haryavana was designated on the coveted post of 22nd Veda Vyāsa.

23. In 23rd Dvāpara Yuga, i.e. 21,605,119 years ago, Vena was designated on the coveted post of 23rd Veda Vyāsa.

24. In 24th Dvāpara Yuga, i.e. 17,285,119 years ago, Vāchaśrava Soma-Mukhyāyana assumed the coveted Chair of 24th Veda Vyāsa.

25. In 25th Dvāpara Yuga, i.e. 12,965,119 years ago,

Tṛṇbindu Tataja occupied the coveted Chair of 25th Veda Vyāsa.

26. In 26th Dvāpara Yuga, i.e. 8,645,119 years ago, Śakti occupied the coveted Chair of 26th Veda Vyāsa.

27. In 27th Dvāpara Yuga, i.e. 4,325,119 years ago, Parāśara Jātukarṇa occupied the coveted Chair of 27th Veda Vyāsa.

28. In the last 28th Dvāpara Yuga, i.e. around 5,119 years ago, Kṛṣṇa Dvaipāyana was known as the 26th Veda Vyāsa.[1]

2000 years ago this day uses to herald the onset of monsoon and the much-needed rains, as the period of Chāturmasya (four months of the rainy season) began from this day. Currently, the rainy season begins from Jyeṣṭha Pūrṇimā.

---

[1] For detail, see pp. 78-86, *Bhāratiya Kālagaṇanā kā Vaijñānika evaṁ Vaiśvika Svarupa*, by the present Author, published by Akhil Bharatīya Itihāsa Sankalan Yojanā, Jhandewalan Delhi.

11

Rakṣā Bandhan

Raksha Bandhan, or simply Rakhi is celebrated in many parts of the India, notably northern and western India, Nepal and Mauritius. Raksha Bandhan means "bond of protection". It is observed on the full moon day of the Śrāvaṇa month.

Actually, annual academic sessions of schools and colleges in ancient India began at the full moon day of Śrāvaṇa, at the commencement of the rainy season after sowing operations were over and crops had begun to sprout up. The commencement of annual academic session was known as Upākarma. According to some authorities or Āchāryas, the full moon day of Āṣāḍha and Bhādrapadawas also considered as appropriate for Upākarma.[2] Upākarma is an abbreviation from Chandasām Upākarma (commencing the study of the Vedas). In modern times, it is also known as Śrāvaṇī Upākarma which is a relatively modern name for this. In early times this period also denoted the Nāga worship performed on the full moon day of Śrāvaṇa, because that too was performed usually on the same day.

With the commencement of the Śrāvaṇī Upākarma,

---

[2] Baudhāyana Gṛhya Sūtra (3.1.2-3); Khadira Gṛhya Sūtra (3.2.14); Hiraṇyakeśī Gṛhya Sūtra (2.18.1)

new students used to undergo Upanayana Sanskāra for starting their studies and old students used to replace their old thread with the new one. The Upanayana thread was considered as 'bond of protection', as in the Vedic culture, the knowledge was considered as the only means of protection and liberation. There is a popular saying in the Vedic culture:

ऋते ज्ञानात् न मुक्तिः ।

Liberation cannot be attained without knowledge.

In Vidura Nīti, it is observed that gods do not protect with a stick like herdsmen. They give wisdom to those whom they want to protect.

न देवा दण्डमादाय रक्षन्ति पशुपालवत् ।
यं तु रक्षितुमिच्छन्ति बुद्ध्या संविभजन्ति तम् ।।

Thus from the foregoing, the discussion it clear that knowledge has a prominent role in Vedic culture and it was considered as the means of protection as well as liberation from the bondage of life cycle.

In Indian historical tradition, bracelets made of cotton used to be tied by the wives around their husbands' wrist going to war as a holy protective shield to guard them against any untoward accident and to emerge as victorious. Earlier these threads were not limited to brother-sister like relationship.

The first reference to this practice is come across in Bhaviṣya Purāṇa. According to Bhavishya Purana, in the war between Gods and demons, Indra ṣdisgraced by the powerful demon, King Bali. Indra's wife Sachi consulted Vishnu, who gave her a bracelet made of cotton thread, calling it holy.[3] Sachi tied the holy thread around

[3] S. Sehgal (1999), Encyclopaedia of Hinduism, Vol 3, pp. 536–537

Indra wrist, blessed with her prayers for his well-being and success. Indra successfully defeated the evil and recovered Amaravati. This story might have inspired the protective power of holy thread.

The second reference is met with Bhāgavata Purāṇa and Viṣṇu Purāṇa, after Viṣṇu won the three worlds from the demon King Bali, Bali offered Viṣṇu to stay with him in his palace, Viṣṇu acceded to the offer. Viṣṇu's wife, Lakṣmī did not like the palace or his new found friendship with Bali, and preferred that her husband and she return to Vaikuṇṭha. So, she went to Bali, tied a thread on his wrist and made him a brother to her. Bali asked her what gift she desired. Lakṣmī asked that Viṣṇu be freed from his words that he would live in Bali's palace. Bali consented as well accepted her as his sister.[4]

Recently, this tradition is associated with Rani Karnavati of Chittor and Humayun. This historical account which dates to 1535 CE is very controversial. Accordingly, when Rani Karnavati, the widowed queen of the king of Chittor, realised that she could not defend against the invasion by the Sultan of Gujarat, Bahadur Shah, she sent a Rakhi to Humayun. The Emperor, according to one version of the story, set off with his troops to defend Chittor. He arrived too late, and Bahadur Shah had already sacked the Rani's fortress. Alternative accounts from the period, including those by historians in Humayun's Mughal court, do not mention the Rakhi episode and some historians have expressed skepticism whether it ever happened.[5] Humayun's own memoirs

---

[4] Prem Bhalla, Hindu Rites, Rituals, Customs and Traditions: A to Z on the Hindu Way of Life, Pustak Mahal.

[5] Satish Chandra (2005), Medieval India: from Sultanat to the Mughals, Volume 2, Har-Anand Publications.

never mention this and give different reasons for his war with Sultan Bahadur Shah of Gujarat in 1535.

From the foregoing discussion, it may be observed without any hesitation and an iota of doubt that with the passage of time the tradition of Upanayana Sanskāra was taken for a formal ritual and the actual significance of Upanayana thread was forgotten. In mediaeval period, the thread of Uapanayana was replaced by the thread of Rakhi and so the Rakṣā Bandhan was also celebrated on full moon day of Śrāvaṇa month after the fashion of Śrāvaṇī Upākarma.

In the earlier period Rakhi was used as a protective shield by the women to guard the men going to war, but in modern times its meaning has also changed and it has assumed the form of a festival to be celebrated by sisters tying threads on brothers with prayers for their well-being, and the brothers giving them gifts and promising to safeguard them at the hour of need.

www.ingramcontent.com/pod-product-compliance
Lightning Source LLC
Chambersburg PA
CBHW021339290326
41933CB00038B/985
* 9 7 8 8 1 8 7 7 1 0 7 2 1 *